lohss NOO-may-rohss: ¿KO-mo say DEE-say? (Spanish)

ee NOO-meh-ree: KO-meh see DEE-chay? (Italian)

leh NAWMbruh: ko-mawnh luh deet-awnh? (French)

numbers: how do you say it? (English)

los números: ¿como se dice?

i numeri: come si dice?

Numbers:

How Do You Say It?

English · French · Spanish · Italian

by Meredith Dunham

Lothrop, Lee & Shepard Books   New York

les nombres: comment le dit-on?

numbers: how do you say it?

First Edition 1 2 3 4 5 6 7 8 9 10

Library of Congress Cataloging in Publication Data
Dunham, Meredith.   Numbers: how do you say it?
English, French, Italian, and Spanish. Summary: Introduces the numbers one to ten in
illustrations and accompanying descriptive words in English, French, Spanish, and Italian.
1. Counting—Juvenile literature. [1. Counting. 2. Picture dictionaries, Polyglot] I. Title.
QA113.D86 1987   513′.2   86-27493
ISBN 0-688-06950-9 ISBN 0-688-06951-7 (lib. bdg.)

For Ellie and Hans Barsch and their many terriers

oon TAHK-see (Spanish)

oon tahs-SEE (Italian)

unh tahk-see (French)

one taxi (English)

un tassì

un taxi

one taxi

dohss pah-YAH-sohss (Spanish)

DOO-ay pahl-ee-AH-chee (Italian)

duh klahwn (French)

two clowns (English)

due pagliacci

two clowns

deux clowns

tray FAWR-bee-chee (Italian)

trwah see-zo (French)

three scissors (English)

three scissors

KWAH-tro MA-nohss (Spanish)

KWAHT-tro MAH-nee (Italian)

KAHtruh manh (French)

four hands (English)

quattro mani

cuatro manos

quatre mains

four hands

SEEN-ko kah-NEE-kahss (Spanish)

CHEEN-kway pahl-LEE-nay (Italian)

sank bee (French)

five marbles (English)

cinque palline

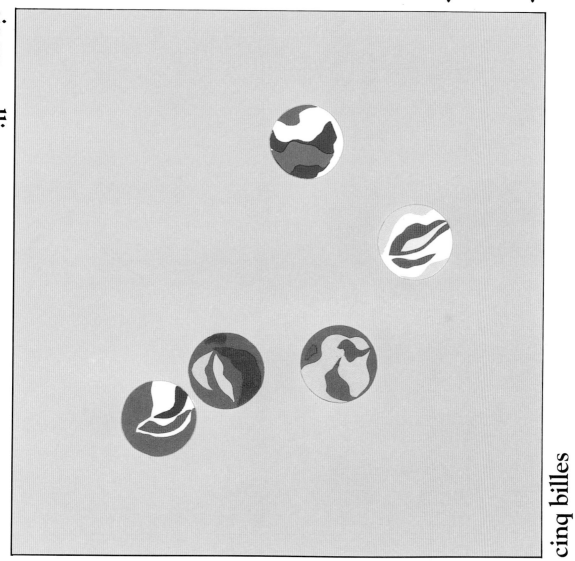

cinq billes

five marbles

sayss PAY-ssayss (Spanish)

SEH-ee PAY-shay (Italian)

seess pwahss-awnh (French)

six fish (English)

seis peces

sei pesci

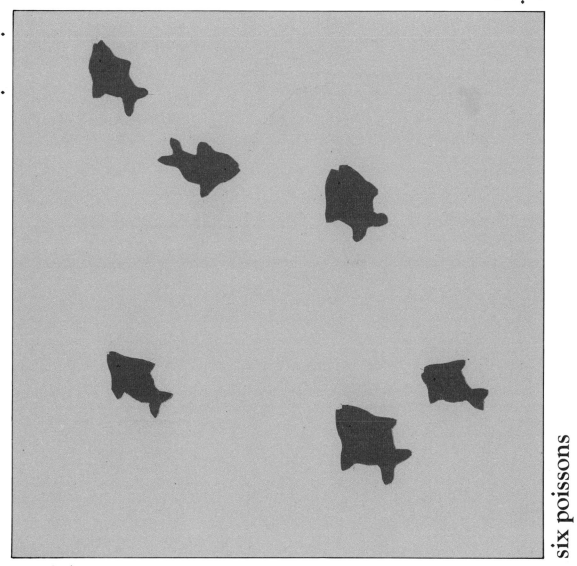

six poissons

six fish

SYAY-tay ess-TRAY-yahss (Spanish)

SET-tay STEL-lay (Italian)

set AHstruh (French)

seven stars (English)

siete estrellas

sette stelle

sept astres

seven stars

eight pencils (English)

AWT-toh mah-TEE-tay (Italian)

O-cho LAH-pee-sayss (Spanish)

weet kreh-yawnh (French)

otto matite

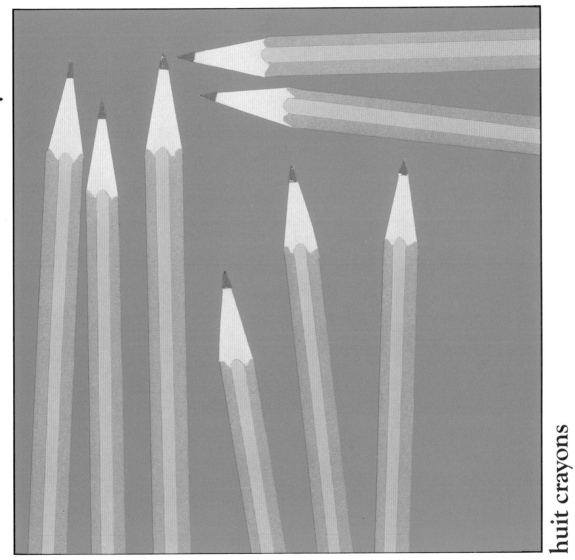

huit crayons

eight pencils

NWAY-vay ess-kah-LO-nayss (Spanish)

NAW-vay gra-DEE-nee (Italian)

nuhf marsh (French)

nine steps (English)

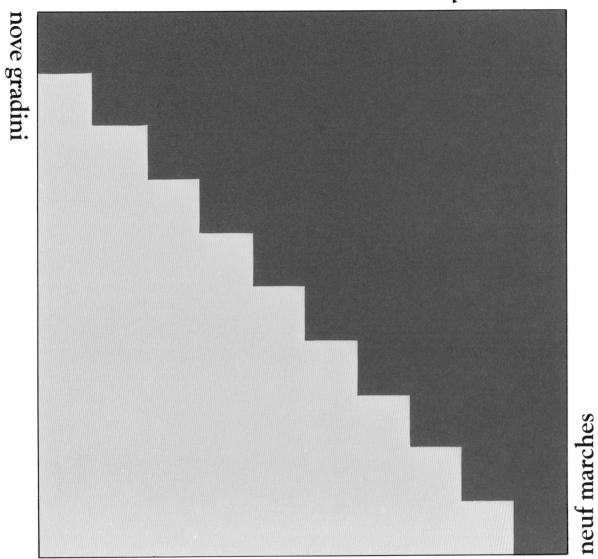

nove gradini

nueve escalones

neuf marches

nine steps

ten seeds (English)

DYEH-chee SAY-mee (Italian)

deess pay-panh (French)

dyess pay-PEE-tahss (Spanish)

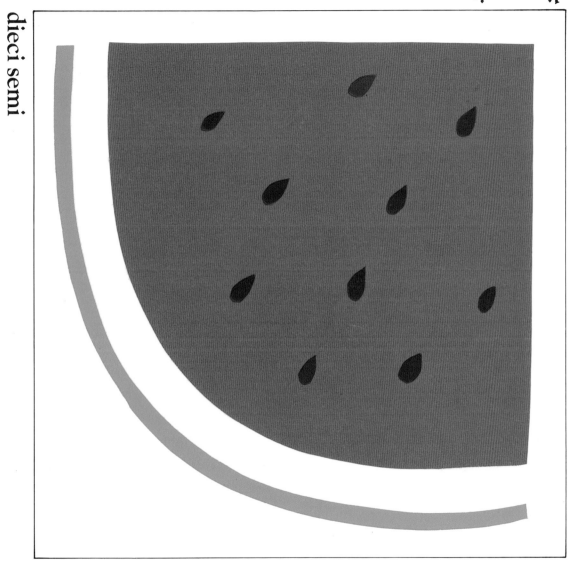

diez pepitas

dieci semi

dix pépins

ten seeds

A Note on How You Say It

Read the pronunciation guides as if you were reading English text, accenting the syllables in capital letters. This will give the approximate sound of the French, Spanish, and Italian phrases. It can only be approximate because each language has some sounds that do not exist in English.

In French, the R is pronounced far back in the throat. The U (represented here as EW) is pronounced by rounding the lips for OO and saying EE instead. The nasal sound represented as a vowel plus NH (like ANH) is made by saying the vowel "through the nose."

In Spanish, the R is trilled with the tip of the tongue. A double R (RR) is trilled longer than a single R.

In Italian, the R is also trilled. A double consonant is pronounced longer than a single consonant.

Many vowel sounds in English are actually combinations of sounds. For example, if you say the word *make* slowly, you will hear EH and EE in the sound of the *a*. In French, Spanish, and Italian, the vowels are pure—containing only one sound.

If you listen to a native or trained speaker of these languages, you will notice other differences. But that's no reason not to have the fun of saying it in French, Spanish, and Italian!